REFLECTIONS IN MY TWILIGHT YEARS:

COLLECTION ONE

REFLECTIONS IN MY TWILIGHT YEARS:

COLLECTION ONE

Creative non-fiction poetry

Karen J. Chism

Heartspeak Publications Incorporated
heartspeakpublications@gmail.com

REFLECTIONS IN MY TWILIGHT YEARS:

COLLECTION ONE

Published by Heartspeak Publications
Incorporated,
Michigan, USA

Acknowledgements

I never appreciated all the hours of work that goes into getting a book ready to publish.

My writing seemed to come easy; with a never-ending supply of ideas from daily life and study of the Bible. To edit my own work, I soon realized was near to impossible. The use of my old, but comfortably familiar "Microsoft Word" program, not to mention the Internet, was a real challenge for me, in my advanced years. Although not impossible; it's difficult to teach this old lady new stuff.

My loving, capable, and very reliable daughter came to the rescue! I gave her so many tasks, she surely deserves the titles: Editor in Chief, Technical Supervisor, Captain of the Punctuation Police, and my Biggest Fan! Therefore it only seemed right; we needed to form a corporation, for without her *co-operation* you would not be reading this book.

Last, but not least, my loving dear husband Jim, so patient! He would find me in front of my computer and wonder when this would be finished. I found myself not able to turn the computer off, but left it on in case I got inspiration in the middle of the night.

Love Ya

I thank my God, through my Lord and Savior Jesus Christ, for the inspiration and the strength to express myself in rhymes.

My prayer, desire, and mission; may all I write bring honor and glory to Him.

†

Table of Contents

<u>What's on My Mind?</u>

It's easier to write, rather than talk these days
Illness has limited my communication ways

I often joke; "I'm every husband's dream"
Most complain wives talk too much, it would
seem

I can express, in an entertaining way
In a page or two, what I have to say

It doesn't take much, to clarify my view
Otherwise boredom, may over take you

The written word, will far out last a quick
answer
My breath it is limited, by the cancer

The positive side is I am forced to think
Does what I'm about to say, really stink?

If worthy I'll think and put pen to paper
My spoken word, disappears like a vapor

If I write it down, it's not expressed in haste
The thought it takes, I don't want to waste

When written down, it's not easy to take back
Perhaps it does force me, to use more tact

Eloquent and fancy words, I don't speak
Writing thoughts, doesn't make me weak

It would otherwise be, just words on my
tongue
I am limited now, with only one lung

My loved ones indulge me; in my new hobby
When asked to review, they are never
snobby

In days gone by, I probably talked too much
When it might have better, just to use a touch

Now it takes more time, to transcribe what's
on my mind
I pray I will be able to express my thoughts,
and still be kind

It helps me to handle the frustration and
stress
And you don't need to wonder, what's on my
mind, or to guess

<u>Tale of the Mysterious Tree</u>

Michigan in December, is a tough time to
move
Endurance and patience, rewards they would
prove

A large unfamiliar bush, encroaching on the
walk
Provided much speculation, and talk

It had white fuzzy catkins; oh, a pussy willow
I guess
It was new to me, but those wild branches
caught my dress

I cut the branches back, from the path to the
door
In a vase in the kitchen, they got compliments
galore
I'd never owned a pussy willow before

A fantastic arrangement, what a display
A God given bonus, I didn't have to pay

A few weeks later, imagine my surprise
The catkins started growing, larger before my
eyes

They changed from white, to greenish brown
It was a sight unlike anything, I had ever found

I researched pussy willows, and none looked like these
I watched in great anticipation, each change a tease

Wait, what is that showing; as the buds keep on growing?
I believe it will be a flower, when it stops snowing

Then in late winter, the large green catkins started to peel
Revealing magnificent magenta color inside; what's the deal?

Each morning I would open, the blinds for a look
Unfortunately, I could not find a likeness in any book

My *spring-starved-eyes*, could hardly wait
I was rewarded, very early rather than late

Imagine my delight, when they began to
unfold
From tulip to saucer, large flowers so bold

Brilliant and perfect in every way
I could not have ordered, more wisely this
day

Deep pink on the outside and bright white on
the top
All over that bush, in glorious color, they did
pop

After the flowers, the dark green leaves did
unfurl
Leaving me much needed shade, as
welcome as a pearl

This was a surprise bonus, of purchasing this
place
The builder made a wise choice, for this
exact space

How could anyone deny there's a Creator?
Oh, the blessing of being a mortal spectator!

The mystery of the unfamiliar tree was finally solved
I just needed more patience, to watch it evolve

Saucer Magnolia is the name of the tree
This amazing bush is a blessing to me

A Song in My Heart

I awoke today, with a song in my heart
Oh what a way, for the day to start

As I stretched my arms, to get the kinks out
All I wanted to do, was give a shout

God has given me, another bright day
To this whatever, can I say?

Give thanks to Him, for the breath I can take
His mercy and goodness, asleep or awake

All the problems today, I think I might face
Pale in the knowledge, of His dear Grace

I think on the things, of Heaven above
I know I am His, and me He does love

The song was very real, it had never
happened before
There was a distinct melody, and now I crave
more

What a difference in the day, my attitude it
makes
My joy, the evil one, he cannot take

I'd let the devil rob me of my song
It is my fault, and I was wrong

I've been quick to grumble, regarding all that
is bad
Not paying much attention, to good, and
that's sad

"Oh, I have so much on my plate," I did moan
"How much more can I take?" Was my groan

I'm not putting my head in the sand
But giving The Lord His place and it's grand!

<u>Recipe</u>

Like a favorite recipe, for dinner tonight
Life needs instruction, to turn out right

Then of course, you need the proper tools
Its results are best, when you follow the rules

When you substitute more for less
Your result will be anyone's guess

I've often referred to the Bible, as my rule
book
As vital for life, as the recipe to the cook

The answer for everything is written in God's
Book
Yet fools plod along, never giving it a look

In your kitchen you made this dinner and it
tasted so good
I thought I was doing everything just as I
should

The problem was I did it my way, rather than
Following your recipe, because I can

Perhaps I thought, no one would know
In my own mind I figured, it was good to go

Don't do as I did, but as I advise you today
Stay close to the instructions or a price you
may pay

Maybe you imagined, you knew a better way
Better even, then God you say?

The result, was only fit for the trash can
Whether cooking or living, you need the right
plan

Some people are better, at following the rules
Some are as stubborn, as mules

Some rebel at instruction, from any source
Some won't even have any remorse

If with dinner you make a mistake, and need
to throw it out
The consequence is not as serious, as what
I'm talking about

The fallout from following, your own desires
come what may
Will yield greater repercussions, along life's
way

To get the best result, follow the instructions to a tee
Of course you have to read **The Book**, that's the key

Branson or Vegas

Branson or Vegas; what's the appeal?
Lakes, shows, and a good meal

Both are noted, for having entertainment
galore
Fun with the family or fantasy with a whore

Patriotic or erotic?
Everything chaotic!

One's full of corn
The other has porn

One has discounts for servicemen and vets
The other will give perks, for high rollers and
bets

A town overflowing with believers
Or losers, boozers, and teasers

One has theaters which thrive on talent and
being funny
The other majestic hotels; built with sucker's
money

"God and Country" is the name of a theater
on Branson's strip
In Vegas you can count on, beauties that
strip for a tip

One promises you variety, of a wholesome
nature in store
The other you can count on, being
approached by a whore

One has more live performances, credited to
its fame
The other is called "Sin City" and lives up to
its name

You choose; *Branson* or *Vegas*, what do you
go there for?
Is it your love of money and you just want
more?

One is surrounded by lakes, hills, wildlife, and
trout
The other by dirt and filth within and without

One can be recounted, as just wholesome
fun
The other just plain wild, two legged beasts
by the ton

One is described, as located in the Bible belt
The other is concerned, with what's below
your belt

Believers or deceivers
Contentment or grievers

One lifts you up; with a promise of a better
tomorrow
The other drags you down, with drink, drugs,
and sorrow

Some might say one is full of prudes
While the other has plenty, of risqué nudes

One you are left, with a goodbye and God
bless
The other you are fortunate, to leave with
your dress

What is the draw, what satisfies all your
dreams?
A chance for riches and chasing after moon
beams?

One talks of fishing and fun
The other tells stories of money won

Both have attractions, which compete for
your soul
One you may leave empty, the other you'll
feel whole

One town makes you want to sing along, with
old fashion tunes
The other you'll be singing the blues, with
drunkards and loons

You choose – Branson or Vegas

Comparing vacations upon return; I hated to
leave, I am quick to report
Their time, went so fast they never even left
the resort

One has fresh air, and God's beauty as far as
the eye can see
The other abounds, with smoked filled
casinos, that's not for me

A town filled with smiling faces, from inner joy
Or a city of sinners, with a clever ploy

Christians that visit Branson, are walking the
walk
Observe the visitors in Vegas, full of sneers
and unsavory talk

A Bible on my coffee table or casino chips in my purse
One filled with a promise, the other a sure curse

Branson or Vegas, *Music City* or *Sin City*
One is just gorgeous, the other just gritty

A life filled with simple pleasures, or sure addiction and booze
Oh, you must see the city that never sleeps; which will you, choose?

The hotel overflowing, with patrons that reek
Hung over from too much fun, they did seek

They can't see a sunrise, over the hills and lake
Their blood shot eyes, the beauty couldn't take

<u>Are we having fun yet?</u>
<u>Quiet! Just place another bet!</u>

Like Len, a "Dancing with the Stars" judge on TV
Wondered, "How three pairs of eyes, so differently could see?"

A Vegas resident thought the desert was so
clean
My trees and flowers to her eyes were as
dirty, as she'd seen

As different as the day is from the black of
night
Two different pairs of eyes, judge what's
wrong and right

Black and White and Shades of Gray

Black and white and shades of gray
Whatever happened to yesterday?

Newer technology gives us more time to play
How do we spend our extra hours in the day?

Black and white and shades of gray

Shooting others with paint balls, might be considered gray
Shooting up with heroin, might be black with hell to pay

How do we discern between black and white
From what source do we receive our light?

What and who, takes priority
Jokes, jocks, and endless TV?

Grandma and Granduncle, have long been gone
Did I spend time, to enjoy their song?

The *"God thing"* people say, "I'm too busy
now and it's for a future time"
But then, how can they get to know, The
Savior that I count as mine?

Texting has replaced, the dear voice on the
phone
Now we put expensive cell phones, on the
throne

That which replaced a face-to-face talk
It's called facebook, and has no regard for
the clock

No need to visit or go out of our way
With all the free time, new technology
promised, what did it take away?

Black and white and shades of gray

Hugs and kisses for a bygone day
Eat drink and be merry they say

For tomorrow you may die
But truly six feet under someday, <u>all</u> of us will
lie

It behooves us to get to know Him
Before our eyes grow dim

It has been said, "Youth is wasted on the young" and "Too smart too late"
Will we stray from white to black and just leave life to fate?

Conditioning, peers, lust, envy, and selfishness is a faker
Getting advice everywhere except from our Maker

When He wants to talk
We need to listen; *often we just walk*

Everyone lives, their life exactly as they choose
Make the wrong choice, and surely you'll lose

Black and white and shades of gray
Right or wrong, who's to say?

Best to stay in the middle
If you want to solve the riddle

We are taught not to take sides
To be everyone's pal, will get you the rides

Surely that is the safest place to hide
"Ignorance is bliss," why in wisdom should one reside?

A little fun never hurt anyone; shades of gray
aren't so bad
A little poop in the brownie; but I'll just
partake of a tad

I wonder does one go from white to black in
one great leap
Or by the road of gray, is it the journey that
you creep?

Black and white and shades of gray
What roads will you travel today?

"Your way is too lonely" she said, "with not
many about
And my friends are all traveling down that
other route"

They say there are "little white lies"
But all lies are black; then trust does die

Boy, you sure can make it tough
The companionship of The Comforter, should
be enough

You can't take it with you when this earth you
will leave
By then it will be too late to see the road; and
you'll grieve

Sunrise–Sunset and Everything in Between

Sunrise—sunset and everything in between
Money isn't the only thing, in this world that is green
The trees and the meadows are so fragrant and clean

From the cradle, we are naturally given to cry
And no one need teach us, how to lie
We don't even need to try

From birth to death, we're filled with what we want
Get it while you can, is the taunt

I need not tell you, that you can't win
For the love of money, will bring all sin

We're urged to go after, this pot of gold
How to hang onto it, we are never told

Be sure to take time out, for what is free
The beauty of a sunrise, over the lake you can see
The early morning calm, is so precious to me

The quiet and still, while all creation sleeps
Not even a bird, yet dares to peep

The sunrise, the new day, God's treasure, the
beginning
While in our twilight, we remember that these,
were worth winning

"Another chapter is closing," my Love with
sad eyes he did say
However our memories, no one can take
away
We have those to dream of, for yet another
day

The beauty of the sunset, over the lake
Brings joy that is dear; no need to fake
This is a gift, only God can make

King Solomon came, to the end of his days,
with this conclusion;
All is but vanity of vanities, and an illusion

Long of years, brings a certain perspective,
we learn
We have no control, over what we earn

All the years we endure the great strife
Only to encounter the emptiness of life

It's not what you can "take with you;" but what
you leave behind
That will be the subject, of your evening mind

Remember, God sees our comings and
goings we are told
He should be our impetus, before we're too
old

Birds of a feather flock together, and all that
are evil know their own kind
But if you don't like your state and expected
fate, change your desires and mind

They say you are what you eat
Likewise you'll wind up, like the friends you
keep

Nothing new here you say,
But remember all those, who have gone
astray

Sunrise to sunset, are the hours we mold
In twilight we should enjoy the fruits, I'm told

Memories of our making
Others will be taking

But their value is untold
Memories can't be sold

Friends

A friend is defined, as a person one likes; and
you claim to have many
I don't know, that I can claim to have any

As the song goes, "What a Friend We Have
in Jesus"
Many will tell you; putting your trust in Him is
needless

He alone is worthy, Him I can surely name
Anyone else, I dare not claim

To me, a friend is more than a casual,
familiar chum
A true friend, when you call, he will always
come

Facebook to me, is such a hilarious joke
Persons claim to have hundreds of friends
and folk

People that have never met you, share their
intimate feelings
With complete strangers you also, share life
changing dealings

I confess I don't get it, I just cannot see
Opening your personal life, to all with glee

Even a chum, of many years by your side
In a wink, he will leave you, at the turn of the tide

Look at Saint Paul's friends, him they did forsake
For Paul to put his trust in them was a mistake

Saint Peter denied The Lord Jesus three times
Rather than risk, being charged with any crimes

But The Lord Jesus will never leave you, His promises are true
Sadly this blessing is bestowed, upon a very few
Some will resist His offer of something new

What friend do you have, that would *die* in your place?
Ask one and they would laugh, or spit in your face

Friends of flesh and blood will continue to fail
In the shadow of Jesus, they will always pale

One way to identify a deceiver
Just compare them to an average believer

They will talk a good game, and promise you
their help
But if things don't go as planned, just listen to
them yelp

The Biblical story of Job, gives a good
example of a friend
One like any of Job's, quickly away I would
send

As for me, I will put my trust in the Lord Jesus
every day
For all my sins; with His life He did pay

Call upon all your facebook chums
As for me; I'll trust The Lord Jesus to come

What would it take for your *friend* to become
an enemy or foe?
I suspect in most cases, just a little dough

You flatter with your words, and they give
kudos to you
Yet behind your back, skullduggery they do
brew

I've witnessed the kisses, and hugs all
around
Just cross them or disagree, and hatred
abound

Proverbs, cautions not to go in their way; join
with them not
If destruction is their game, your soul it will rot

They will "friend" you and invite you to *like*
Be careful, it is not you, at whom they will
strike

I've seen it happen, all in the very same hour
One was praised and then quickly, they tried
to devour

They will make a snare and dig a pit; your life
to take
Maybe it will backfire, their plan, will He
break?

Even when your heart, toward The Lord is always leaning
You need to rely on His strength; you can use His intervening

Your own enemies, surely you might not be able to overtake
With His help, maybe no progress will they make

It will always be done in His will, I can say
Whatever He decides, with me it is okay

The Long Goodbye

Oh, how exciting is love when new
Moments spent away, are very few

Two different people growing together with
God's direction
Makes for a marriage, of blissful perfection

As time marches on, hardly a private thought
in our mind
It's the blending by love, ideas of the same
kind
The need for explanation, is rare these days
we find

We learn what the other's wishes and desires
are
We make every effort to satisfy them by far

Now my body grows weak and the mind
likewise for he
Put the two parts together, makes one
wonderful new we

Memories we once shared, begin to fade
away
The illness has stolen, our yesterday

These times they are hard and not much fun
But, strangely I treasure, each and every one

Even though we have lost much of our former self
God's mercy toward us, is of tremendous wealth

Which of us will be the first to go?
No one but God can really know

Our time we gladly, put in our Lord's hand
His will be done, and it will be grand

His will is best; mine makes a mess
His has already been put to the test

If it's ok with Him, it's ok with me
For I'm told we will still have eternity

We can't dwell on what we had, that's no more
But I look forward to the blessings God has in store

<u>What's for Dinner?</u>

"What's for dinner?" my love asked of me
— *"What do you feel like eating?" I asked of he*

"Oh, I don't know, whatever you want," was his reply
—*There's some stuff in the fridge, maybe we can fry*

"Would you rather go out, to a restaurant instead?"
— *"I don't know. Where do you want to go break bread?"*

"I don't know, what tickles your fancy?"
— *I hate to try anything new tonight, or be chancy*

"But there's a new place that just opened up down the road"
— *"I don't care, is that the place to me you showed?"*

"It looked kind of clean and neat"
— *Maybe that's a good place to eat*

Oh, I don't know . . . round and round we go!

"Guess you're not very hungry if you can't decide"
— *"No "got to have" hankering, in you does abide?"*

"Maybe you're right, so you go ahead and decide"
— *I can't think of anything, I've tried!*

"Let's call Chuck and Carol, maybe they will go"
— *A different place, they might know*

That's fine with me...so call them and see

I rang them up to inquire
Only to get deeper, in questions and mire

The same problem at their house I did find
Neither of them, could make up their mind

"Perhaps that new café," Chuck suggested to her
— *We just went there last week, but it's all a blur*

"Whatever y'all want, is fine with me"
— *I'll find something on the menu, happy I'll be*

"We can meet you at five, or is that too early?"
— *"I need to fix my hair, to make it curly"*

By this time we were all too tired to go
Maybe we'll try again next week, and take in a show

So, my love and I, took out of the fridge
A few things and we each had a smidge

Survival or Excuse

Survival today, is synonymous with "ya gotta do what ya gotta do," but what does the phrase really mean?

Webster defines survival as, *alive you remain* Modern language has changed it to; *give one free rein*

Okay, what would you do to *survive/remain alive*?

How far would you go?
Or, what would you keep a secret; and what would you want God to know?

An example can be found, in a record of the Bible, 2nd Kings – Chapter Six Cannibalism of the most shocking sort, you will find in the mix

But is that really a fact?
Remember, Jeffrey Dahmer, surely you've heard of that!

There is nothing new, this side of Glory

There was a great famine, recorded in a
Biblical day
What is the necessity today, would you say?

Money could only buy an ass's head, or a
dove's poo
Yet today you proclaim, "Ya gotta do what ya
gotta do"

Dog eat dog is now *acceptable*, if you want to
get to the top it's the rule
"Ya gotta do what ya gotta do;" might you use
killing for a tool?

It's your *standard of living*, you strive to
maintain
Is there no limit, to the others you blame?

In the courtrooms today, everything is a
disorder, and therefore a killer might win
Or, is lust and covetousness, what drives us
to sin?

The path in the end that will cause you to
lose
In God's eyes you'll just sing the blues; <u>you
choose</u>

An old saying; *"you never miss what you never had"*
But a case of *the greens* will make you sad

Envy is the cause, of our resentment and strife
These feelings I promise, will cut like a knife

When we set our mind to thinking it's owed to us, by the Feds or Uncle Sam
Don't be surprised when their laws, down our throat they will jam

We are in effect, anointing a King
And he will surely, give us the "bling"

Survival is based, on just enough to remain alive
Not a standard of living, to match one out of five

I think *survival* today, sports the political attire
The wearing of an evil, destructive desire

We are taught and programmed, to create
A *must-have* we attempt, to legislate

We need to discern, our *needs* from our *wants*, and what is our duty
Maybe it's time; we don't take another's booty

Many passions, we have been able to mask
as our right
We will steal from our kinfolk, when the going
gets tight

Luxury masquerading as needs, when it isn't
necessary at all
But who will be the judge, to say how much is
enough or too small?

Some will argue, so and so has it so rough
So let's make the rich, find out just how tough

We are all born equal; ready to take, take,
and take
We holler and cry, for that which we didn't
make

Well let's make the *haves*, take care of the
have-nots
They won't even miss it, they have lots

After all you say, that so and so has more
than they need
So to survive I need theirs, you will plead

They claim to have looked and worked; and
everything they have tried
"But nothing has changed," or so they cried

If you claim you *survived*, it means you have *remained alive* and made it
But some will complain "I gotta do what I gotta do," and they pitch a fit to stay out of the pit

The *pit* for one person, might be a tent
Another might complain, of the high rent

Is true survival, the subject matter?
Or, is this argument, more political chatter?

Well it must be the government's fault, or this political party or that
It is not fair, that some should have more then they need to get fat

"Ya gotta do what ya gotta do," is the mantra and the buzz
Is this God's plan, or man's way that it was?

But the world is evolving, you object and demand
I ask, "So who do you want in command?"

On TV this morning I learned something new
Three women were defending "what they gotta do"

They are stripping in clubs; it's all about the
money they holler
In this economy, in *gentleman's* clubs they
can make top dollar

"After all they have children to feed," they
said in their defense
To all three of them it makes perfect sense

More to my point, I took exception when they
went on to proclaim
They were doing this all to further the Gospel
in Jesus' name

Yes, I was shocked but not regarding their
job
But that they claimed the name of my Savior;
that made me sob

So I see this world spiraling downward,
further every day
If contrary to the Gospel in the Bible; it's a
different way

To get what you want, you need to elect a
president or anoint a king
After all, here and now, God won't let you
have everything

"Ya gotta do," is a popular colloquialism of today
But it is not a very accurate description, I say

You do not *gotta;* I think you just *wanna* have an excuse
For objectionable actions that maybe you produce

Duchess

My nest was empty, there was a real need
Someone, something, to care for and feed

My Love said, "A little Yorkie; if we get a pet"
I jumped at the suggestion, first chance I
could get

I told my Love, the range of how much one
would cost
My, but they are expensive, hope it's not
money lost

He agreed to a price, right smack dab in the
middle
All that just for a pet, which often did piddle

While visiting out of state, I found a good
breeder
Better jump at the chance, and not teeter

That evening I asked my Love, "A male or a
female?" did he prefer
But I promptly chose a spunky puppy, without
his confer

In the morning I called, and announced with some fear,
"It's a girl honey, what should we name her?"

I told him she pranced and she danced around like a race horse; her head held up high
"Duchess!" he exclaimed for a name; surely she will rule our home by and by

When I brought her home, my health was not the best
Let me tell you, a new puppy will put you to the test

I prayed daily for The Lord, to give me strength to endure
For my Love and I wanted, to be able to keep her for sure

For seven years now, she has ruled our home
We are her servants, not far from her dare we roam

Duchess makes sure her "subjects" are not out of sight
A tiny little dog, thinking she possesses great might!

She has brought into our life, untold pleasure
Joy and entertainment, without measure

Surely, a Yorkie is one of God's gifts to
treasure
She must be just the smartest doggie ever
I can't tell you how very clever!

She can understand, what we are talking
about
We are just learning, what this means without
a doubt

When you have to spell out a word, so
Duchess won't know
It's just a matter of time, she will master that
and it'll show

All who meet her fall head over heels in love
I know she is our special blessing from above

In Grandmother's Eyes

Oh, you are just the cutest one yet
Never has there been another like you, I bet

He's the best, the most perfect ever
There isn't any joy like he brings, not any
ever

Look at that dimple, pretty as can be
You know, she got that from me

She just learns to do everything quicker
If I needed to, I would surely pick her

If he's fussy, it's only because you failed to
learn baby talk
Perhaps you'll understand him, by the time
he does walk

My kids were never as smart, as my
grandchildren are
They are way ahead of their parents by far

Oh! Did I show you the photo? Ever so cute!
She doesn't crawl, but she does scoot

All the smarts came from my side of the tree
It's in our family genes, you see

That bad thing that he did today
Comes from your Grandfather's side, I say

He can do no wrong, in my eyes
Those other kids, how they must lie

She is talented, way beyond measure
To me, an unspeakable treasure

I can spoil him; for it gives me great joy
To be able to buy, yet another toy

It's my prerogative, my right; don't you see?
I then send them home, they'll not bother me

It's really fun, to have them around
Makes me feel young, more alive, I've found

It's amazing how easy it is to teach
something new
Mistakes they never make; well, just a few

All those stories you tell me, of the times he
acted up
You must be doing something wrong, yup

When they are at my house, they never fight
Must be because Grandma, is always right

Mom and Dad don't know anything; they never did
Until they grew older, and no longer a kid

Then they understood, how wise their parents are
Smarter than any, of their friends by far

If there is a conflict, I'll always take their side
When in my presence, they get a free ride

God must have made grandchildren, for spoiling
He gave Mom and Dad, the chore of toiling

A gallon of love and a jigger of correction
That's all it takes, to end up with perfection

It's more fun to be a grandma, than it was a mother
Leaves all the responsibility, to the other

Easy for Grandma to give the advice
Ultimately Mom and Dad pay the price

Save your breath Mom and Dad, you know you can't win
In Grandmother's eyes, your children don't sin

<u>Johnny Made Me Do It</u>

It never was a credible excuse, and still isn't
today
To blame someone else, so you don't have to
pay

An "*addiction*" has absolved, your
responsibility for the deed
I'm shocked even the law, lets you legally
plead

Modern psychology has allowed, an abuse of
the diagnosis
To put sin in the same category, as a
neurosis

If we can put onto perverted behavior, a label
Then insurance becomes available, and
payable

There is no diagnosis, no medical billing
code, for common sin
But thanks to our decadent morals; we can
justify, condone, and win!

"I couldn't help it; I had this condition," you
say
"Pardon me, my debase character got in the
way"

A pervert that prays, on innocent girls and
boys
The little ones they reduced to, nothing but
toys

All manner of evil, is now described as "*sick*"
Therefore we pity, rather than convict

Vulgar, corrupt conditioning, is the order of
the day
That gives you a pardon, for your selfish way

How the guilty, become the victim, in my
mind I do weigh
The trend away from God, is responsible for
conditions of today

If in a movie, or even a book
From the worst of life, the story it took
Have you noticed the star, is always the
crook?

A disease is a condition that impairs one's
mind
It legitimizes all corruption, of any kind

Void of decency, but filled with self
While, God's word collects dust on the shelf

I was astounded to hear, on the news today
A pervert's attorney wants the city to pay

The obscene mayor, didn't get proper
instruction they say
The tax-payers' money we'll take, that's in
vogue, and is the way

Why do people put up with all the white
washing of crime?
You can bet it's because, the majority are of
the same mind

It's a disorder, a sickness; like diabetes they
cry
But really the heart, never dares to ask why

How passionately one will fight, to take credit
for the good
Yet do all in their power to transfer the blame
for bad if they could

It seems it's man's folly, to think they can
make better
A world that was designed, to follow God's
letter

Let us be the judge, let us decide what is
right
But between us, all we ever do is fight

We've been told what is expected, of us for
today
But rebels we are, trying to do it our way

Since Adam and Eve, the first family God did
make
One brother wanted, what was not his to take

"It's my life; let me live it," you say
"Then when things go wrong, I'll have others
pay"

Johnny made me do it; someone else can
take the blame
It seems like little Johnny, is destined for
fame

The Clock

Tell me why the hands of the clock on the
wall move so fast
I know they moved ever much slower, in
times past

The older I grow, the slower I move
The clock's hands travel faster, something to
prove

The chime says, "It's time to get up"
But didn't I just have sup?

I can't seem to finish, all that I've planned for
the day
That evil clock just ticks on, and gets in my
way

When a fun thing is planned, and I check the
hands again; they never moved
Then all my efforts to rush them, will be stuck
in the grove

Tick tock, it pays no attention to my wants
I will do as I please, it seems to flaunt

Oh, why does that clock want to give me trouble?
I need more time for the same thing, even double

What I used to accomplish, that clock gave me an hour and a half
It seems to be watching me, taunting with a laugh

If there was some way that I could slow it down, to make the hands obey me
Then I'd have no problem finishing, the tasks at hand, you see

It's not my fault; I purchased a racing clock for the wall
The label didn't explain, all its pit falls

I'd take the clock back, and purchase another one
But I'm told they all follow the pattern of the sun

The answer I guess, is to be happy doing far less
Changing my goals, might cause me less stress

I've talked, with other elder folks regarding
this beef
Seems they all bought their clocks, at the
same store of grief

Fast Talking

Why do young people talk so fast?
I understood not; to repeat, I had to ask

It is annoying, especially on the phone
My husband won't even talk, and he's not
alone

To understand, only one word out of three
I will have to assume, what you just said to
me

That's not a good thing, might even be a
tragedy
Mistaking the meaning, of your words might
be a calamity

Thought you said, you were on your way
But, you told me to make it another day

My Love he did ask me, "What did they say?"
I'm not sure, but I think they are on their way

Dinner was on the table, at the prescribed
time
The only plates cleaned, were his and mine

I take pity on you, and blame my *old ears*
But my advice is, when not talking to your
peers

Learn to slow down, and speak more clearly
For all the older folk will thank and love you
dearly

I've given up trying, to watch a DVD
Unless it has closed caption, for me to see

It's just as infuriating as movies were before
"talkies" were made
Trying to figure out the dialog, before
showing the next frame, it does fade

Please help us out, and pretend you are on
the stage in a play
Wanting all in attendance, to understand
what you say

One day you'll understand, what's so irritating
to me
If you live long enough, perhaps you'll make
the same plea

If the newscasters dared talk like you do
The viewers, I promise you, would be very
few

Take an old lady's advice and learn
something important today
Bet you will find a better job, even with more
pay

Live and Let Live

What exactly is your thought when you utter
the expression "live and let live?"
This is a common retort, and advice some
may give

With a shrug of your shoulders, and perhaps
you say, *"Whatever"*
Anything and everything it seems, is
accepted as clever

Saw a youth slug an old lady in the face
None of my business; I'll not give chase

Stay uninvolved and don't offer any help
Don't even bother to give a good yelp

Are we moving toward the permissive society
of victim-less crimes?
Where no one is right or wrong; is *sick* a sign
of the times?

The bully, that slugged the old lady, is of a
certain class
It is society's fault, so give him an excuse and
a pass

When everything is okay and just a matter of life
It conditions us to accept everyday strife

Spoilers

Everyone's desire I'll bet
Is to get all of the answers, yet

A course in philosophy, we'll take
Surely smarter this course will make

Understanding we'll then attain
Happiness and riches we'll gain

Tradition some say, is the course to follow
The advice learned; we're sure to swallow

They say it is sure to make us a winner
No matter if we stay a sinner

Wisdom, knowledge, and fame
This is the desire of all; everyone's aim

If we don't get it, then who can we blame?
Money and time spent, it's a shame
No one ever taught the need to ask, "In His
Name"

*But from the Bible we can learn a different
way*

In God and Christ all the treasures are found
But "hid" to be discovered in the pages thus
bound

Perhaps we have studied from the wrong
book
Maybe we should take another look

Understanding all the wisdom stated in here
It will take *way* too much effort, we fear

After all, a good job it won't get; we see
From all that wisdom we'll just flee

We're told we must seek out the very best
school
If we're to acquire the proper tool

Our profession while here on this earth
The financial rewards, it will never be worth

After all, this life won't last forever
Our talents we'll put forth, in this endeavor
Ah, but <u>they</u> are the "spoilers," clouding the
truth forever

The *spoilers* of the more *perfect way*; are
deceitful vain traditions and philosophy
These subjects are contrary to God, as we
will see

The very best schools are trying to remove
Any mention of a Creator; His existence they
try to disprove

Upon God's plan they say they can improve
But attention to God and His word would
behoove

The traditions of men are the enemies of the
Cross
This will result in our greatest loss

Spoilers will draw us away from the truth
Their target is always our gullible youth

Spoilers will always seek out a feeble mind
We need to use our *God given glasses*, the
truth to find

To gain a seat in the class of God's Word we
should seek
We may be shunned by the popular clique;
even labeled a geek

Therein can only be found, wisdom and
Christendom
Teaching from our Creator's curriculum

It's never right to do wrong or wrong to do
right;
Our reward will be basking in God's glorious
light!

Practice Makes Perfect

Keep on, keeping on; the same direction and actions of your own will
You're sure to attain your goal and your desires still

Just follow the lusts of your own heart and you will gain
You are sure to acquire a spot in this world to reign

Just follow the early example of Cain
The results undoubtedly, will be the same

God may even send you a delusion; to believe a lie
But God also may give you up, if the lie you do buy

Just keep at it, living your own way
God promises in the end you will pay

Even here and now in this life, you may be aware
This road you are on, is not without care

The promises of God; or the inclinations of
Satan; which will you follow?
The truth of His Way; or of Satan's evil fraud;
will you swallow?

Practice makes perfect, and proficient you
will be
Establishing your fate after this life you won't
see

Fill yourself up to the brim with whatever God
calls sin
In anger, hatred, wrath, drunkenness, and
such, you'll never win

Conditioning is evidenced the more you
perform
After conditioning sin will become the norm

Do it once and it will become easier the next
time
Do it over again, you will be blinded to the
crime

You will become an expert in deception
You will be your own worst enemy without
exception

Practice and you are sure to get it right
Just remember you are never out of God's
sight

Defense

A teen was driving stupidly drunk
The legal system today, gave an excuse for
this punk

He was suffering from the "*disease*" of
"*Affluenza,*" therefore he was excused
The attorney and the judge justified, the
excessive booze

The perpetrator killed four people, and
forever altered the life of another
By his "**defense**," he was justified; sin it did
smother

This kind of "*defense,*" puts the blame on his
parents
Saying they gave him an abundance of
money; therefore, were errant

These days psychiatry claims, too much
money is to blame
When it is given in place of morals, it's a
shame

But the downside of this label of "*Affluenza;*"
does say
In the place of responsibility, the killer doesn't
pay

After all he never was schooled in wrong or
right
It's not his fault, so the court can't indict

Too much money put more stress on this
wealthy brat
Daddy's money will buy an excuse for that

Therefore; he is not to blame for drinking and
driving
He will be allowed to be free; unlike the dead,
he's alive and surviving

He will not serve any time behind bars
Sentenced to probation, ignoring the victim's
scars

Shame on the attorneys and shame on the
judge!
What parts of our laws did they expertly
fudge?

An abundance of wealth is now to blame, for drinking and driving he did care less
This poor "*little rich boy*," had to ease the stress
He has a legitimate "**disease,**" I guess

You can now murder, rape, and steal; committing all manner of sin
Just retain the right counsel, and in court you will win

But there is a greater Judge who will adjudicate someday
Woe to all those fools that believe, a contrary way

***The more we remove God and His rules
The more power we give over to Satan
and his tools***

Thank You

~~~~~~~~~~

Thank you so much for reading this book.

It was a challenging but satisfying experience to publish my first collection of poems, so they could be shared with others.

If you are reading this page, I hope it means you enjoyed my rhyming enough to read to the end. If that is the case, I would be extremely honored if you would tell others by writing a review on the retailer's website where you purchased my book.

Additionally, I hope you will look for Collections Two and Three of the "Reflections in My Twilight Years" series; release date, spring 2014.

Thank you again and God bless,

Karen

~~~~~

If you would like to receive updates
concerning future offerings by Heartspeak
Publications Incorporated or this author,
please send an e-mail to:
heartspeakpublications@gmail.com
asking to be added to our mailing list.

~~~

Heartspeak Publications Incorporated
Logo design by: K. Compton

www.ingramcontent.com/pod-product-compliance
Lightning Source LLC
Chambersburg PA
CBHW020516030426
42337CB00011B/408